# THE BEST DOCTOR WHO POEMS IN THE UNIVERSE

Edited & compiled by Garry Vaux

Published in Great Britain by

GJB Publishing

Printed by in Great Britain


All Rights Reserved



Copyright contributors 2011



Doctor Who © BBC

GJB Publishing
18 Yeend Close, West Molesey, Surrey KT8 2NY
www.GJBpublishing.co.uk
feedback@GJBpublishing.co.uk

# Introduction

Welcome to the first ever book of poetry and art dedicated to one of THE greatest television programmes ever – Doctor Who.

Poetry isn't an area normally associated with Doctor Who but this small yet perfectly formed collection may just be the start of a new adventure for Who-related poetry.

The series has produced stories with a whole spectrum of emotions so poetry would seem an ideal medium to explore and I hope it will encourage others to give it a whirl.

I'd like to thank all the fans from all four corners of the globe who have contributed poems for this book and also for the illustrations sent in, which I'm sure the Ninth Doctor would describe as "Fantastic!"

There's a variety of subjects including The Master, Rose, Donna Noble, The Green Death, Cybermen, Sarah Jane (which is sadly more poignant now) and even the Doctor Who magazine gets a nod!

A special mention must go to Gregory Ovenden, Paul Bensilum and Philip Thompson who managed to incorporate Raxacoricofallapatorius in their poems and also to Steven Evans who devoted his entire poem to this neighbour of Clom!

So vent the thermo-buffer, floor the helmick regulator and dive headlong into this collection of Doctor Who poems. Geronimo!


Garry Vaux

# Contents

# The Doctor and Rose

by Andrew Binny. Australia

There once was a man who travelled afar,
Through the future, history and to the furthest star.
Though the thing that he sought and tried to find,
Was someone to accompany him and would not mind.

Many companions he had through an adventure or two,
Some stayed a long time and some for only a few.
Some that found him and some that he chose,
Until finally he met the one they called Rose.

She was to him a caring friend,
One that would help him out until the end.
One that saw the weakness behind his lonely eyes,
And heard the silent voice that cries.

And in return he grew quite fond of her sight,
Showing her the stars and a long ago won fight.
But whatever they did and wherever they went,
They both seemed to enjoy the time together they spent.

When danger threatened and reared its head,
He sent her away though she did see red,
And she did all she could to get back to him again
And that she did, to save him from pain.

But in the end came the time to depart,
No time to say what was in their heart.
The destruction of a sun was a small price to pay,
For one last chance to be able to say:

"I..."

# Ten - an obituary

by Monika Berberich. Germany

The Tears of a Time Lord

So precious and rare

Take ages to drop

This life was not fair.


The Lonely Angel

Of Flesh and Bone

His hearts saw too much

Must turn into stone.


A machine for Time

A Box full of Space

'The Laws became mine'

Yet marking his days.


He cannot resist

Sad Man in a box

A moment he missed

Four taps, then four knocks.


A creature in snow

The Golden Glow

A whisper at last -

I don't want to go...

# The Master

by Andrew Knight. Southampton, UK

You've heard of a cad called The Master,

Who loves shrinking folk with his blaster.

Well the problem he's found,

When The Doctor's around,

Is his plans always end in disaster.

# The Doctor's Disaster

by Bethan Williams

The starman sails in the waves of the sky.
The doomed walk the decks of a sinking ship.
Drowning in air, they are losing their grip.
Helpless starman, you'll watch them all die.
Disaster will strike, it can't be denied.
The balance of power has finally tipped.
You're floating to death in a fiery crypt.
You can't save them from this: say goodbye.

Time is running out-
No.

I am no starman.
I am the fire.
I am the ice.
I am the rage of a thousand suns.
I am the beginning.
I am the end.
I am all of eternity.
I am ancient.
I am forever.
I am Gallifrey.
I am no starman.
I am the answer.
I am the Doctor.
Got a problem with that?

# An Unearthly Child

by Brad Truran. Sydney, Australia

In London, a Shoreditch junkyard is

The unlikely hideout of a TARDIS

Barbara and Ian

Can't believe what they're seein'

And get whisked off in Space-Time. Quo vadis?

# Dream Doctor

by Charles McGrath

---

Red locks sway in the mournful breeze,

As life continues, the same it's always been.

But not forever, not for a while,

Not with the man of her favourite dreams.

The blue box opens,

And there she stands,

Amongst caverns of gold,

With that legendary man.

But a dream it is, nothing more,

For the red-haired girl, she dreamt of war -

Strife on Earth,

An army of hate,

All crying continuously,

One single word - 'Exterminate!'.

Yet more creatures have come and gone,

And over time their hearts did bond.

From the spaceman and his startled 'What!?',

To Donna Noble and the days she forgot.

# Farewell, David Tennant

by Dan Mason (15) Rhode Island, USA

After being poisoned by radiation, 10 was in a horrible state.

Because it was lethal, it sealed his fate.

He went back in time to see all of his friends.

And the relationships he could, he tried his best to mend

Before the radiation forced him to regenerate.

# Who am I?

## By Robert Cocking and Ben Brown

I am the Doctor the man of many faces I have been to many
times and places I have seen galaxies planets and stars from
Skaro to Varos and the planet Mars.

Abound from planet Gallifrey, scared and alone 2 hearts inside
me that beat as one
On the run from my people, in the TARDIS my home
The hero and savior of the human race I see danger and try to
make the universe a better place.

No matter the danger, the 11 heroes stand tall
The Cybermen, the Daleks, I strike fear in them all
If you are trapped and in a no win position.
I will stand before you, this mighty apparition.
Many of my loved ones, my companions, my friends
They never give up always fighting to the end
The selfless act of this superior being
Is evident for all and quite clearly can be seen
But the underlying reason to eradicate the badness
Is to mask the truth, to hide my inner sadness
For I'm the Doctor, scared and alone
The one and only time lord, with the TARDIS my home.

# Metal Mutt

by Scott Montgomery. Dundee, UK

There was a dog called K9,

Who loved to travel in time.

When the Doctor's in a rut,

He calls on this metal mutt,

And everything works out just fine.

# Untitled

by Gregory Ovenden

From Raxacoricofallapatorius,

Dealing with Slitheen can be laborious,

Masters of disguise,

A family so monstrous,

Only Time Lords or Febreze could be victorious.

# The Watcher

by Gregory James. Swansea, UK

Draped in the darkness in the corner of the room,

Where even colour is too scared to hide,

From the murky grey, ZOOOM –

Two eyes! Watching me – but I cannot see

My body is quantum-locked – it cannot turn from the brink

Of the chair, and My eyes, my eyes stare –

I cannot blink! Cannot blink! Must not blink!

It's there! There – over there!

Don't turn around – if I turn around...

On the screen, pulling me in – the vortex swirling

Hurling out colours and shadows and - what's that!

Maggots and monsters. Ideas and fears. Laughs and

Real, real tears. And then laughter again, excitement – shooting

Back through the tunnel, faster and fast a blinding light!  The light,

My wife has flicked back on – "Look at you, watching Doctor Who –

You're like a little boy, perched on the edge of the chair – you couldn't take

Your eyes off it – you haven't had your tea!

Who would have thought it – you're 43!"

# Green Green the Death

by Andrew Hampel & Sean Wilson (New Magnet)
Yorkshire, UK.

'Twas in the town of Llanfairfach
Where darkened times did choose
To encase the place with the loss of life
And the death of the minor Hughes
'Twas near the global chemicals plant where His body lay serene
But his passing brought a mystery
As it glowed a deathly green.

I dwelled within the Wholeweal,
The nuthutch to another,
We lived in our community,
Sister, father, brother,
And as we ate fungal protein, A message from the mine
A man they called Dai Evans,
On his life they had called time.

The green death's what we called it,
Formed from the chemical age
And carried by monster insects
In their larval stage.
Professor Jones searched for a cure
He tried and tried and tried,
But he caught the emerald curse
And very nearly died.

Through an act of serendipity
an antidote was discovered
And Nancy she made sandwiches
As Professor Jones recovered.
We all ate fungal protein
It's tastier than meaty faggots
And we all recall the episode
The one with the giant maggots.

# Run

by Ian Lucas

---

Out of the living room
And into Saturday night

Out of breath
Out of space
Out of time.

Hearts beat palms sweat
Breath
-less
Into your nightmares
Out of control.

Corridors, chalk pits, upstairs, downstairs
Over the cliff and under the ocean.

From here to there
And back again
Into danger and out of sight
Into the future and out of the past
Another place, another time.

Hold my hand and run.

# History Repeating Itself..?

by Jamie Austin

Show saviour
"Magic" retainer
Reputation restored
Fans applaud
Programme shaper
Rumour maker
Doctors cast
Reference the past
New themes
Pre-title scenes
Faster plots
Late timeslots
Interview grins
Forty-five mins
Fan scripts
Overseas trips
Comedy turns
Companions return
Costume chooser
Doctor loser
Gap year
Ratings fear
Singing assistant
Fans resistant
Starry casts
Ailing fast
Stayed too long
Is he gone?
Series wrecker
(that Double Decker!)

# Untitled

by Kate Green. Sutton, UK

---

Lord Nimon knew that death loomed,

So he ranted, and he roared, and he boomed,

"Bring me Hymetusite,

My shoes are too tight!"

Soldeed cried, "You're all doomed!"

# Untitled

by Kate Green. Sutton, UK

---

The Master's first tale is fantastic,

The aliens are animated plastic!

The Time Lords unite

UNIT and daffodils do fight!

It all sounds a little too drastic!

# Sonnet for a Human

by Kendra Bergstedt. USA

My love is lost and so I say to thee:
I can still feel her, beating in my hearts.
I have survived to be nine hundred three:
I knew that we would always come to part.

She came by chance, there hiding in the dark,
I saved her life and took her for a ride.
At first we were upon a simple lark
Before she chose to never leave my side.

We saved so many people I've lost track.
My brains, her wit- we made a perfect team,
Afore she fell off of my life's steep path.
I'll never see her face again, it seems.

But I should say that not a flower grows
that can compare to my beloved Rose.

# Doctor Who Englyn

by Leslie McMurtry. London, UK

Do come, tune Wales to Doctor Who today,

Parfait TV debut,

So-named show of sonic screw-

Driver: revered rendez-vous.

The englyn (pl. englyionn) is a complicated form of syllabic Welsh poetry. There are many types, with different sets of rules. This is an example of the englyn cyrch, which has seven syllables, with lines one and two rhyming, and line three cross-rhyming with one of the syllables of line four.

Dustin Wilson

Dustin Wilson

Peter Bolt

Kendra Bergstedt

Jamie Austin

Jamie Austin

Peter Bolt

Andrew Merkelbach

# BLINK

by Shawn Scott Smith. Asheville, NC, USA

Sally Sparrow, Don't Blink,

Never shut your eyes, not a wink,

Angels of stone creeping,

Stay vigilant or end weeping,

Sent to the past, your friends all gone.

Listen for the TARDIS and its brilliant song.

The doctor running with bow in hand,

Such a wonderful, curious man.

Now remember Sally, no matter what,

Don't blink, don't wink, no eyes shut!

# Waiting for Who?

by Matthew Lidbury

After Christmas Day, the programmes did pale;

My remote dusty and unloved - forgot.

No spinning vortex, hero; and no fight,

No reason to switch on; cower in fright.


I cast back to battles in time and space,

And projected Time Lord out from my home.

I pictured in my mind his earnest face,

And closed my eyes hoping to hear him come.


With growing glee Spring came - my faith did grow,

A Police call box seen with fresh blue door.

With bated breath I thought what winds would blow

would I see Ood at song, monsters at roar?


The mighty Doctor's in - all's well once more.

I've learned. Patience is certainly no flaw!

# The Doctor and his Companions

Matthew J. Shochat. Boston, USA

He travels in a blue box

Ran away from Gallifrey

Legacy of travelers

Barbara, Susan, Dodo,

Nyssa, Jaime, Vicki,

Donna, Polly, Martha, and

of course Rose Tyler.

He has faced terrible foes;

Daleks, the Master, Cybermen,

Satan, Autons, the Alliance,

and the Weeping Angels.

His home is lost in fire,

War that ravaged spacetime.

He is the intergalactic

Hobo who makes things better.

# Delia Derbyshire

by Pauline Sewards

We are in one of those places that isn't quite anywhere -
The hard shoulder of the M62
Retuning the radio, the sound comes through in querulous spikes -
The voice of Delia Derbyshire
Syncopates the night.

She did her work back in the sixties,
A Sasooned and mini-skirted Goddess of Geeks.
Only years later got credit due
She was with Oram and Grainger
In the Radiophonic workshop but

Delia wrote the music to Dr. Who.

Images of outer space
Recall those long ago Saturday egg and chip teatimes
When Delia's multi phased sonic innovations
Reeled us in to the tingling Science Fiction comfort zone.
Fractal patterns breaking in a world where identity slips
And time trips over and over

She was the Queen of synaesthesia
If you can have synaesthesia in black and white.

And now we are stuck in this car on the highway,
If we could see through the fog
To the other side of the motorway
We'd be watching our younger selves
Coming the other way.

Is it interference in between stations?
Or does the voice of Delia Derbyshire
Syncopate the night?

# The Touch of the Mara

by Paul Bensilum. UK/Taiwan

I enter the silent darkness,
Chimes leading into dream time,
Nothing now, just emptiness,
Laughing echoes down my spine.

The Mara bares himself before me,
Naked and vulnerable our souls unite,
For a fulfilment he pleas,
For release and flight.

We entwine and snakedance
Knowing all the moves, like chess in the dark
Satisfaction shows in his glance,
Now that I bear his mark.

The sensual feel of pure evil,
Snaking deeply throughout my body,
Too powerful for most people,
I savour its touch deep inside me.

Banished by those who could not understand,
My forbidden desire of great horror,
Deep within me his return is planned,
For I am one with the Mara.

And one day I will release this evil snake,
He will be universally victorious,
Debauchery and sin he will make,
From Earth to Raxacoricofallapatorius!

# Evolution of the Cybermen

## by Rod Tame

The public might scoff but a boffin states

"Cybermen will exist one hundred years from now".

Technically possible, technically-evolved humans - Wow!

Is it me? Or might this be unwise?


With medical implants,

These next-gen men will have senses enhanced.

But Mr. Scientist, please, use your common ones to see

The drawbacks in this plan.


People living lives extended,

Like a clapped-out banger

Having body parts mended,

Does not help solve the over-population conundrum

Or the pension fund doldrum.


Not to mention the intention

Of these mechanic fanatics to rule the world - FOREVER!

Have you NEVER watched Dr Who?!

If you had, you would agree

The obvious conclusion to your scientific spree.

This upgraded form of life

Would declare the likes of you and me

Obsolete - like analog TV.


Mother Nature's organic spawn

Would, at best, be sub-species pawns.

At worst, a faded blast from the past.

Extinct in the blink of a cyborg's eye.

Except it probably won't blink.

Professor, stop and think!


But not about how to pioneer this crackpot idea.

When tinkering under the biological hood,

Do you ever consider whether you should?

# Memorised

By Matthew Exell

The first thing I remember,

Aged three, is mummy's face:

Bandaged, blank.

Mummy's cold embrace -

Calmly killing a man.


In school some books were targets.

I took aim - they helped me

Learn strange words:

'Ass-ass-in'; 'Ye-ti';

'Gen-e-sis'...of a nerd.


I've lived with it for years now,

Subscribed to odd routines:

Thud on mat –

This month's magazine!

Three decades loving that.

My son fears Angels' embrace,

But enjoys my old school.

Loves his mag -

Same as this old fool -

And words like 'cy-ber-mat'.


One fear we both remember:

A half dead assassin,

Scary, mad,

Who - about to win -

Wound up being not all bad.


Will I recall how I die?

Embrace or T.C.E?

Will I smile

As, at death bed scene,

My Doctor tends a while?

# Eleven - so far...

by Monika Berberich. Germany

A prison, a cage
A monster in rage?
A Mad Man, a tale
Then Silence, so pale...

A bitter sweet Song
For The Lord of Time
So near, soon gone
Yet he will be thine.

A secret, a mystery
A puzzle, a game?
Both dead and yet living
Hold on to his name.

The merry child:
She does not know
What's growing inside
A Beast Below?

The box and the wife,
A graveyard of shells
Hello to Goodbye
Once more, a Farewell.

One Eye so mild
She's guarding so keen
The fearful child
This must be the Dream!

# Oh, Raxacoricofallapatorius!

by Steven Evans. Cambridge, UK

Oh, Raxacoricofallapatorius,

Your name throughout space is simply notorious,

Your people are gross, but your climate's quite glorious,

So sad, Raxacoricofallapatorius.


Oh, Raxacoricofallapatorius,

There's blood on the wind from the hunters' victorious,

And Slitheen/Blathereen so vile and cantankerous,

So sorry, Raxacoricofallapatorius.


Oh, Raxacoricofallapatorius,

With trees made from fartzwood that grow thin and tall-ious,

Your oceans a-swarm with beasties gi-normicous,

Oh poor Raxacoricofallapatorius.


Who gave you a name so frankly absurd-ious!

# Drums of the Master

by Alies Bruinsma. The Netherlands

The sound of drums.
Awakening in my head.
Volume increasing.
Slows to drive me mad.

The sounds of drums.
Drumming louder in my head.
No longer to drive me insane.
Shaping revelations instead.

Destruction awakens.
Worlds disappear.
While the drums keep on drumming.
And I smile about those who fear.

The planet keeps on screaming.
Fighting all along.
But the earth is already whispering.
Singing the end of it's song.

And I...
I play the melody.

**Tadadada... Tadadada...**

# I'm Not Me Anymore

by Thomas Hey. Bradford, UK

Dying of old age, a body so frail,

Forced by my own, placed in exile,

Exposure to crystal, a push by K'anpo,

Falling from a, radio telescope,

Just one antidote.


Banging my head on, the ship's console,

Shot in the street, a mistake in the hospital,

Lost in the time war, all a bit vague,

Vortex absorbed, an innocent saved,

Radiation delayed.

# My Lady of Sorrow and Tears

by Steven Evans. Cambridge, UK

I brush the souls of countless lives,

A soft caress so swiftly gone,

And then I touched a kindred mind,

That filled me with love's endless song.


So young and fresh, so full of fire,

A stainless blade, a mystic knife

Which cut the chains that bound my hearts

And warmed the wasteland of my life.


Through danger and adversity,

Beyond the Pale of cosmic night,

Our spirits joined in one accord,

Our joy and pleasure burning bright.


Yet chaste our love, our friendship pure,

No stain of impropriety,

We two together evermore,

A foolish dream, as now I see.

Eternal, yes, Death's power I spurn,

Her form so frail in Time's dark hand,

She born of Earth, I of Gallifrey,

The human shell, as soft as sand.


Desire I hid, buried feelings deep,

And broke her heart when I set her free,

Returned to a world built of empty dreams,

Where the stars call her name and will not let her be.


Sarah Jane,

Whom I left so alone through the years,

Sarah Jane,

My lady of sorrow and tears.

# Sad Man's Box

by Vanessa Aisha M. Singapore

Never a word was goodbye,

As she said she was alive,

Until the moment that she would die,

Until the moment that he would cry.


Two ancient souls who roamed the universe,

Had an understanding that always was,

And as they parted in epic sadness,

Hello would crumble into dust and tears.


And so for her to leave he did not want,

Centuries awaiting this timeless dance,

So clandestine was his life,

So was hers she was his wife.


And would they meet once again,

When they ended both in pain,

Yet continue they will to travel,

And through time and space they'll see the world.


(Doctor Who S06E04 The Doctor's Wife)

# The Doctor's Theme

by Vanessa Aisha M. Singapore

Hark can't you hear him he's dying.

The music that breaks the essence of my soul,
It speaks the feelings I cannot hold.
Beneath the crystal clear droplets of rain,
Lie in stillness on the wall of the window pane.
I see the stars enveloped in the universe,
An epic song of freedom that always was.
It hides beneath the eyes of a single person
With haunting rhythm the eerie voice of the siren
Ignites the doomsday I have felt for so long,
It is the only one I will remember the only song.
Across the darkness the life among the distant stars,
I will cross the worlds to find where you are.
No longer the dream of a normal death,
Seek the adventures there's something left.
This is our world, our childhood, our home,
Next stop everything where love don't roam.
When I say vale decem it's not goodbye,
I hear violins and piano in the night sky.

Hear the Doctor's theme I am not crying.

# Doctor Who and the Motorway of Time

by Philip Edmund Thompson. Worcester, UK

One day, our Time Lord was doing swell

Polishing up the Cloister Bell.

When suddenly it began to bong.

Something outside had gone seriously wrong!

"What's happened, Doctor?" Nyssa asked

As Tegan drank some tea from a British Airways flask.

"The TARDIS has stopped in mid-flight," came the reply

"I'll switch on the scanner to find out why."

With a whirr the screen revealled

A sight so astonishing that their eyes refused to yield:

Rows upon rows of time machines,

Some in plain sight, others virtually unseen.

The Doctor explained "From what I can gather on the Index File,

It looks as if we might be stuck here for a while.

The line stretches from the 28th moon of Sirius

And ends past Clom, a planet near Raxacoricofallapatorius."

"This part of the Vortex of Time and Space
Is like a dual-carriageway limited access highway for time traveling races
With machines less complex than the TARDIS, you see."
"Oh great, a futuristic M1!" Tegan moaned as she poured some more tea.


"Brave heart, Tegan, no need to whine.
We're just in a traffic jam on the Motorway of Time.
If I dematerialise the TARDIS and increase the trecipidation
I should bypass the jam and materialise her to the nearest service station."


Which is why on that day in the Crystallined Lodge
A Time Lord and two humans laughed, realising they've managed to dodge
The entire Motorway Police Service with an old Type 40 TT Capsule so fine
As they ate Sol 3 cheeseburgers and drank fruit juice squeezed from a Lollopian Vine.


The moral of this poem? It's not a whole bunch of gammon:
Not everything can be fit into "Doctor Who" canon!

# Seasons of Gallifrey

by Maximilian Curtis. USA

In the winter, the children of the Shining World
Would slide down sloping valleys
And dance in the rippling ice fields as the tides drew closer.
> Smoldering in the ashes, a dead world turns round its black sun,
> And the whispers and legends of ages linger in silence.
> Some still sing of that world, the war, and all they had lost;
> But only in memory can that burnt orange sky be rekindled.

In the spring, rivers would swell over great floodplains,
And iron hawthorns gently swayed
Beside molten rushes at the water's edge.
> From their citadel the Lords observed every star that ever was,
> Forever confining the rage and majesty of Time.
> They watched the galaxies below with ancient eyes
> As the heavens shimmered with beautiful chaos.

In the summer, those alien sands settled at the shoreline,
And the cries of strange birds wheeled in mountain mists,
Echoing down to crystal groves and the gates of Abydos.
> Children entered the Academy, and soldiers emerged.
> For glory they marched into the virgin fire,
> And for untempered bloodlust they burned the cosmos,
> Returning resurrected and slaughtered and forgotten.

In the autumn, a second sun would rise in the south,
And silver leaves would catch its light like liquid steel,
Beneath a burnt orange sky that never was.
> Ashes smoldered in the pit, and the immortals became gods,
> Though their hearts had grown cold and weary.
> The Shining World burnt brighter than ever before
> As it faded slowly in requiem for the undying night.

Sometimes eternity is no time at all.

# Whispers in time (Legend of the Doctor)

by Jacob Davies

You'd day dream and wither your life away,
If it weren't for that man from Gallifrey.

He'll whisk you away to faraway lands,
Always stopping to lend a hand.

To anyone, no matter the colour or creed,
He just likes to help those in need.

Fighting monsters and demons that go bump in the night,
His reward is adventure at dazzling heights.

Take his hand, travel through the whole of forever,
And always count on him to say something clever.

As the both of you stare death in the face,
Never wanting to give up the thrill of the chase.

He's simply a hero, one of his kind.
He'll never leave a good person behind.

# The Delight Before Christmas

by Sebastian J. Brook

'Twas the night before Christmas and all through the land,
we wait for the TARDIS, all blue and so grand.

The shopping is finished, well, as much as we could,
Quick! Down to the pound shop, where Woolworths once stood!

A toy from last year at a bargainous price,
So what if it's plastic? It still looks quite nice!

It's a gift for my uncle, who lives far away,
In the constellation of Kasterborous, the planet Gallifrey!

It exists in a time loop, hard to get to, you see,
There's a Taxi that goes there, with a quite hefty fee.

I'll send it by Reindeer, with my old friend, Saint Nick,
He'll get there in time, with a neat little trick.

He'll slide down the chimney (Yes, they have them there too),
They have them on Skaro! (but ought really not to!).

But the hour gets late, and to home we must go,
Through the crowds and carols, and the impending snow.

To a place by the fire, with the Quality Street,
Or the Cadburys Roses, or anything sweet!

And then off to bed, where tomorrow we'll find,
A room full of presents, from people so kind.

Skip forward six hours, to quarter past three,
We're full up from Turkey, and all the debris.

But in two hours from now and 45 minutes,
We'll be sat all together, watching Doctor Who, innit!

The one with some Dickens, some singing and sharks,
It's written by Moffat, and will be full of such larks!

So we raise up a glass to all fans as we write,
Happy Christmas to all, and to all a good-night!

# Time Loop

by Gerald Riley. Surrey, UK

In the constellation of Kasterborous,

There lies a special place.

Locked in time through the spoils of war,

One survivor - who changes his face.


He's lived for over nine hundred years,

But perished after four knocks.

His name is heard throughout the universe.

This mad man with a box.


So whenever you travel in time and space,

Through the stars so wild and dangerous,

Listen for the echo of two beating hearts,

In the constellation of Kasterborous.